the **Victoria Vox**

Original Songbook for 'Ukulele

ISBN 978-0-9801283-0-7

P.O. Box 66625
Baltimore, MD 21239

cover photo by Karen Sandler

America

from "Victoria Vox and Her Jumping Flea"

**Words and Music by
Victoria Vox**

Ukulele Tuning:
G-C-E-A

America

America

A - mer - i - ca   A - mer - i - ca _____

Pack   up   the   car_____   turn   the   ig - ni - tion.

Buttercup

from "Chameleon"

Ukulele Tuning:
F#-B-D#-G#

**Words and Music by
Victoria Vox**

Buttercup

Buttercup

photo by Samuel Bramwell

photo by J.L. Okray

C'est Noyé

from "Chameleon"

**Words and Music by
Victoria Vox**

Ukulele Tuning:
F#-B-D#-G#

C'est Noyé

mer   il ya le vent, le   soleil___   et si j'ai du___ mal   C'estNoyé,C'estNoyé_____   je   et je

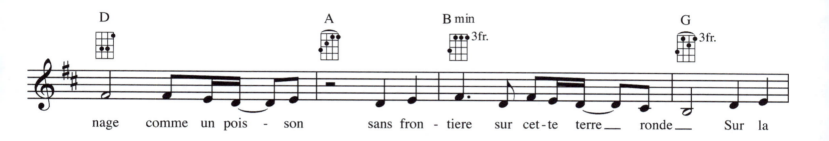

nage   comme un pois - son   sans fron - tiere   sur cet-te   terre___ ronde___   Sur la

mer   il ya le vent, le   soleil_____   et si j'ai du___ mal   C'est Noyé, C'est No yé_____

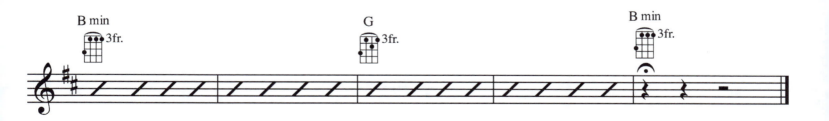

Christmas With You

from "Victoria Vox and Her Jumping Flea"

Ukulele Tuning:
G-C-E-A

**Words and Music by
Victoria Vox**

Christmas With You

Dreamin' 'Bout You

from "Victoria Vox and Her Jumping Flea"

Words and Music by
Victoria Vox

Ukulele Tuning:
G-C-E-A

1. I've been dream - in' 'bout you.
2. I keep think - in' 'bout last night
3. (solo)
4. verse 1

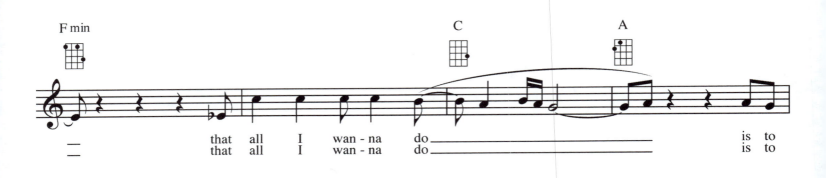

You keep run - nin' through my head don't you know babe,
with your arms a - round me tight don't you know babe,

that all I wan - na do is to
that all I wan - na do is to

fall in love with - a - you!
get (back) in bed with - a - you!

Dreamin' 'Bout You

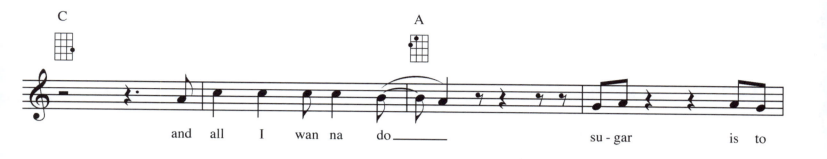

and all I wan na do_____ su - gar is to

fall in love____ with - a - you!____

Jessica

from "Chameleon"

Ukulele Tuning:
F#-B-D#-G#

Words and Music by
Victoria Vox

Look-in' a-round the room for some thing to do for a piece of truth

May-be I'll fly to space where I can live my bet-ter days

whoa

Jessica

Looks like I'm a mess under stress but don't you for-get
You've got quite the nerve to be cal-lin' here kick-in' up dirt

I've got a heart of steel ain't noth-in' like ach - i - les heel whoa ___ My
Why don't you live your life in-stead of livin' through mine

heart keeps beating and I know that I'll be fine ___ I ___ don't know why ___ you ___ come ___ round here I said my

heart keeps beat ing it's in time ___ so I ___ don't know why ___ you ___ come 'round

here oh why you come a round

Jessica

Jessica

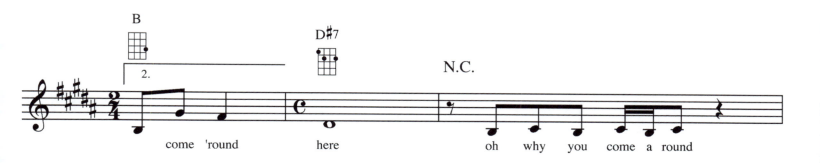

come 'round   here   oh why you come a round

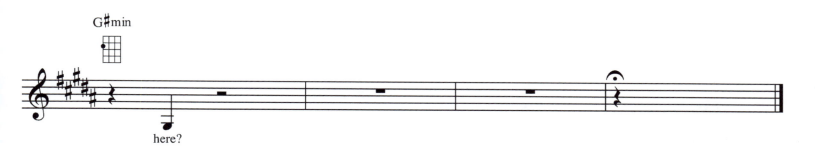

here?

My Darlin' Beau

from "Victoria Vox and Her Jumping Flea"

**Words and Music by
Victoria Vox**

Ukulele Tuning:
G-C-E-A

When the sun 'll rise ____ I think I know what ____ I'll find, my dar-

- lin', oh My ____ Dar - lin' Beau. ____ We

laid love on the line ____ un - der the moon late ____ last night my dar-

My Darlin' Beau

photo by LAUNCH

photo by Scott Habicht

Peeping Tomette

from "Chameleon"

**Words and Music by
Victoria Vox**

Ukulele Tuning:
F#-B-D#-G#

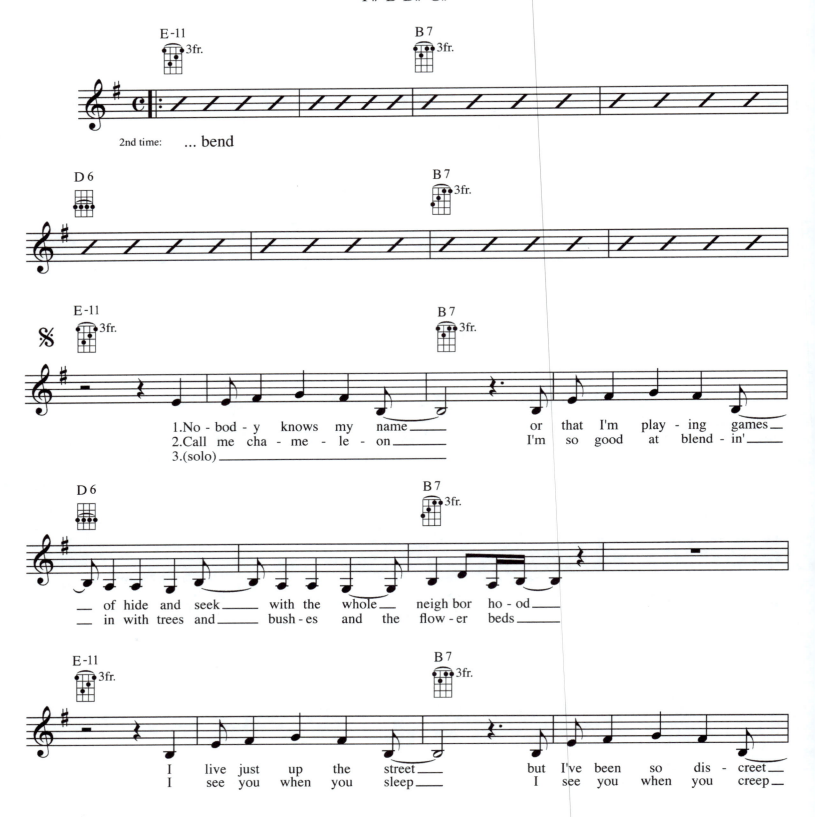

2nd time: ... bend

1.No - bod - y knows my name ____ or that I'm play - ing games ____
2.Call me cha - me - le - on ____ I'm so good at blend - in' ____
3.(solo) ____

__ of hide and seek ____ with the whole ____ neigh bor ho - od ____
__ in with trees and ____ bush - es and the flow - er beds ____

I live just up the street ____ but I've been so dis - creet ____
I see you when you sleep ____ I see you when you creep ____

Peeping Tomette

Peeping Tomette

The Bird Song

from "Chameleon"

Words and Music by
Victoria Vox

Ukulele Tuning:
F#-B-D#-G#

I'm gon na sing _____ sing like a bird _____ a bird in the sky ___

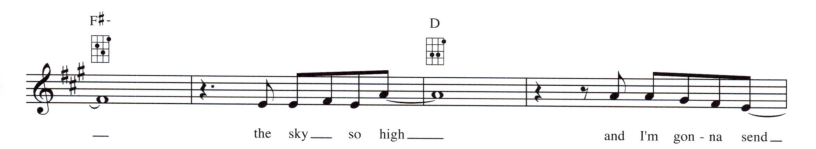

___ the sky ___ so high _____ and I'm gon - na send ___

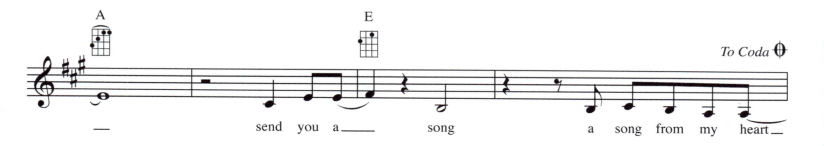

___ send you a _____ song a song from my heart ___

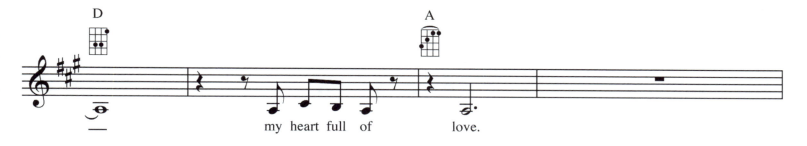

___ my heart full of love.

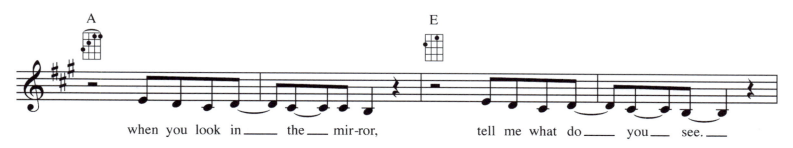

when you look in _____ the ___ mir-ror, tell me what do _____ you ___ see. ___

The Bird Song

Do you see___ me ___ in your eyes?___

al-though I can't be ___ there ___ ev-er y ___ day

you can ___ hear ___ me ___ if ___ you ___ try ___ 'cuz I'm gon na sing

heart my heart full of love ___ a song from my

heart my heart full of love.

Tucson

from "Chameleon"

**Words and Music by
Victoria Vox**

Ukulele Tuning:
G-C-E-A

The

des - ert is___ too hot___ for all this cold - ness in my heart___ I
sing - in' here___ in town___ to - night, I won - der if you'll show,___ or

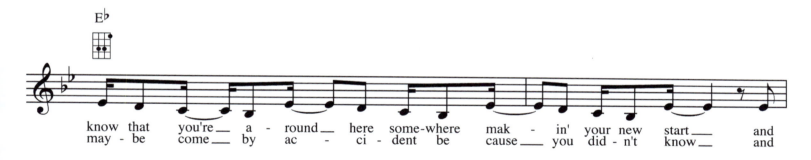

know that you're___ a - round___ here some-where mak - in' your new start___ and
may - be come___ by ac - ci - dent be cause___ you did - n't know___ and

ev' - ry corn - er that___ I turn I wond - er if I'll see___ and
list - en to___ the songs___ that I have writ - ten a - bout you___ and

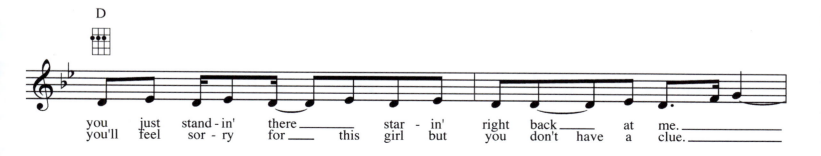

you just stand - in' there___ star - in' right back___ at me.___
you'll feel sor - ry for___ this girl but you don't have a clue.___

Tucson

Tucson

Tucson

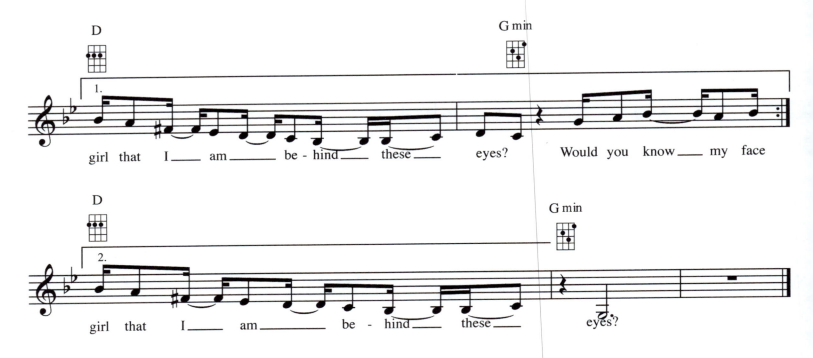

girl that I___ am_____ be - hind___ these___ eyes? Would you know___ my face

girl that I___ am_____ be - hind___ these___ eyes?

Ukin' at the Wheel
(Runnin' From the Law)

from www.youtube.com/victoriavox

Words and Music by
Victoria Vox

Ukulele Tuning:
G-C-E-A

Got my ped - al to the med - al I'm
Sor - ry Sher - iff can you tell me where is the

run - nin', run - nin' from the law_____ A
prob - lem with Uk - in' - at the Wheel?_____ I

dang - er - ous la - dy with my u - ku - le - le, the
don't want no troub - le in my tin - y bub - ble, it

Ukin' at the Wheel
(Runnin' From the Law)

bad - dest that you ev - er ___ saw ___
real - ly ain't a ___ big ___ deal ___

Driv - ing down the high - way,
I tried to warn the pub - lic,

steer - ing with my knee you think how could it be 'cause
to save a life, ___ all my tour dates are on line ___

I've got my ped - al to the med - al I'm

run - nin' run - nin' from the law ___

Ukin' at the Wheel
(Runnin' From the Law)

I'm run - nin' run - nin' from the law____

I'm run - nin' run - nin' from __ the law! _____

What's Wrong?!

from "Chameleon"

Ukulele Tuning:
F#-B-D#-G#

**Words and Music by
Victoria Vox**

What's Wrong?!

Yodelayheehoo

from "Victoria Vox and Her Jumping Flea"

Words and Music by Victoria Vox and Stolie

Ukulele Tuning:
G-C-E-A

Yodelayheehoo

me   and my   Yo - del - ay -   hee -   hoo._____   (Who?!)   I   said it's just

me   and my   Yo -   del - ay -   hee -   hoo. _____

Biography

Victoria Vox may not have had much of an audience as a 10-year-old, but that didn't stop her from writing and recording her first songs in her bedroom in small-town, Wisconsin. Vox has always known it was her destiny to perform, but didn't find her true voice in performing until after tackling a Casio keyboard, violin, oboe, trumpet, guitar, bass and now, ukulele.

Missing her junior prom in high school, Vox traveled overseas as a foreign exchange student to rural France where she bought her first guitar. A new instrument and an inspirational environment turned her away from her keyboard top-40 musings and band-geek rut, encouraging a more therapeutic and purposeful songwriting method.

Vox continued her higher education at Boston's prestigious Berklee College of Music. A degree in songwriting was right up her alley, plus, the male-to-female ratio was 6-1! Meticulous about honing her craft, the then pink-haired "conservative" punk-rocker worked on tweaking her songs, and was later rewarded in the form of a Berklee Achievement Scholarship and the Vince Gill Songwriting Award.

After graduating in 2000, Vox moved to Nashville, TN, but rejection from the holier than thou exclusive Country songwriting community pushed her to carve her own path. She decided to dodge the grits, sold everything she owned and jumped the pond to London, England. Six concentrated months later she returned to the states with a collection of emotionally inspired songs, which fell into place on 2002's gorgeous acoustic memoir, *Still*.

Too anxious to wait for a break to come her way, and encouraged by the positive fan response to her first two CDs, Vox finally took the plunge. In May of 2003, she quit her "not-at-all-missed-retail-job" in Green Bay, founded her own publishing company, Obus Music, and took to the road full time, sharing her songs and infectious smile from Los Angeles to London. Shortly after teaming up with midwestern singer/songwriters, Stolie and Kellie Lin Knott, to form the acoustic trio, Tres Femmes, Vox picked up the bass and first debuted her ukulele.

In November of 2004, she recorded her own guitar and bass tracks on *(in between)*, an EP of catchy pop songs layered over looped drum samples. The new disc sold like hot cakes on a rush of tour dates through the East Coast and Midwest, but with folks eagerly begging for an album of ukulele songs (which they heard at the live shows), the ground was set for Vox's next big move.

In February of 2006, Vox released *Victoria Vox and Her Jumping Flea* to rave reviews. On her first Hawaiian tour in support of the album, Vox was offered sponsorship by KoAloha Ukuleles out of Honolulu. *Jumping Flea* has been featured on NPR's "To the Best of Our Knowledge", the song "America" was used on A&E's Random 1 and indie film *Lost in Woonsocket*, and "My Darlin' Beau" was awarded runner-up in the International Acoustic Music Awards. She also received ASCAPlus awards for being an active writer outside of broadcast media.

In the fall of 2007, Vox completed her follow-up album, *Chameleon*, with an early 2008 release date, and for the first time mixed her ukulele ditties with the guitar songs on one album. For the past 4 years, Vox has been performing full-time across the continental U.S., Hawaii, and Western Europe in a wide range of venues from theatres to coffeehouses and festivals to living rooms.

For live videos, music and more, visit these sites:
www.victoriavox.com
www.myspace.com/victoriavox
www.youtube.com/victoriavox

Song Map

Yodelayheehoo

the bird song

Tucson

what's
wrong ?!

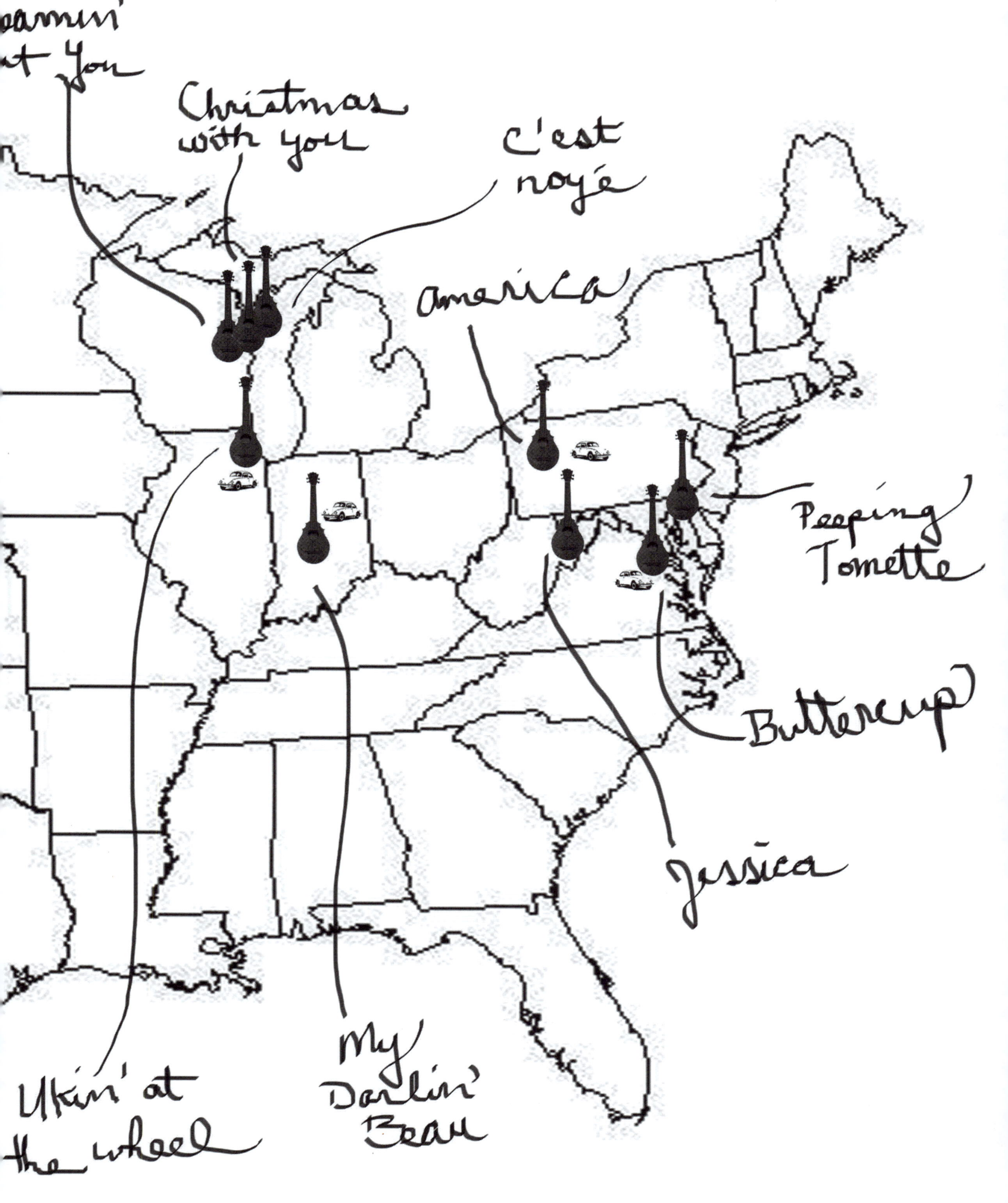

Dreamin'
at You

Christmas
with you

C'est
noyé

america

Peeping
Tomette

Buttercup)

Jessica

Ukin' at
the wheel

My
Darlin'
Beau

NOTES

NOTES

NOTES

NOTES

THANK YOU.

Ukenited We Stand ;)
Thanks to all my ukulele playin' friends all over
the world! I really appreciate your support.
A Big Mahalo goes out to KoAloha Ukuleles,
Jim and Liz Beloff, Karen Sandler,
Mike Tarantino, Stolie, and Mike Noonan.
Thank you, Mom, for teaching me how to use
Photoshop :)

And... Thank YOU for strumming along ;)
Uke On.
xoxo
Victoria Vox